General Hooker in the Civil War, later, had "Each corps, division & brigade designated by different badges & standards, so that their respective commanders could pick out their men in action or upon the march" in 1863, General Mottocks tells us in 1903. An equestrian statue had just put up in Boston, honoring General Hooker. Such is the reason for the flag that follows, that of the 2nd Massachusetts Cavalry & their California 100, who were known to be fantastic riders.

Arms of California, a Grizzly Bear rampant bearing the American flag, furled to denote peace, was submitted by Lt. Joseph Revere, USN, 1848. He was the grandson of Paul Revere (from whom he learned heraldry) and was nearly "on the spot when the Bear Flag events took place." On July 9, 1846 in Sonoma he replaced the Bear Flag with Old Glory (see the cover of Vol. 3 of this series) and his Bear Crest honors the earlier flag and those who raised it. He noted, too, with some pride, "the trade of this country has been mostly monopolized by a few Boston (trading) houses, and Boston is better known among the natives of all kinds than any other part of the United States."

TUEBOR

I will defend

See the flag of the CALIFORNIA HUNDRED, further on:

Also see Vol. 3 for Lt. Revere's full Arms for Cal.

none are extant; the source is poet Rogers' 100-page epic *The California Hundred*, 1865, where it is often described in detail. Poetic license? Hardly, with saintly Thomas Starr King their leader in San Francisco, it is surely truthful. There were "hundreds of battle flags" *(Whitman)*, most bloody and lost. A regimental flag, not a mere guidon, was needed, and the design with both states' emblems was appropriate and historic. Ask Mr. Bear here, and Lieutenant Revere.

THE WIDE-AWAKES PARADE UP MONTGOMERY STREET FOR HONEST ABE,
San Francisco, 1860, thousands of uniformed members, marching at night by torchlight,
protecting anti-slavery speakers. Their message: they would fight to END SLAVERY!

Flag: Univ. of Hartford

California spared
from the Civil War:
GENERAL ALBERT
SIDNEY JOHNSTON,
the Loyal Traitor,
1861

When the Civil War broke out, many secessionists wanted to try to take California out of the Union. Gen. Johnston was in command of the Department of the Pacific, with headquarters on Bush Street, San Francisco; he was an ardent secessionist. Gen. Twiggs, in command in Texas - Johnston's state - took Texas over to the rebels. There was fearful pressure on Johnston to do that here. "But Gen. Johnston was a man of the nicest sense of honor, and refused to betray the trust he held under his commission." Gen. Sumner came after a while and replaced Johnston, who surrendered his command and commission. "No one can contemplate without horror the awful conditions which could have arisen on this coast if Gen. Johnston had yielded to the entreaties of the extreme secession element. The whole state and the adjoining territories would have been deluged with blood. Cities and towns would have gone up in smoke, and California would have been reduced to a howling wilderness. Thanks to Johnston's nobility of soul, our state was saved from a calamity which would have brought sorrow and mourning to thousands ... Let no man mention this great captain's name disparagingly." - *Ayers*. Johnston was soon in command of the Confederate army at Shiloh, the bloodiest and most decisive battle of the war. In front was Gen. Grant, who said later that only Johnston's death had saved the Union army there.

See Ayers, *Gold & Sunshine*, 1922

Federal, left: dark blue coat and trousers. Gold epaulets, belt & buckle; buff sash; brass buttons.

Confederate, right: gray coat with buff collar and cuffs; gold sleeve braid, gold wreath & stars. Buff sash; brass buttons & belt plate; light blue trousers.

CALIFORNIA,
FISHING & LUCK:
JAMES C. FLOOD
& WM. O'BRIEN,
SAN FRANCISCO,
1861

Jim Flood & Bill O'Brien, who ran
the Auction Lunch in San Francisco,
went fishing by Goat Island, filled
their boat with salmon, and
returned with fish for all. They led
a cheering parade with fife & drum
and a big American flag. As they
marched down Montgomery Street,
hundreds more joined in. The heroes
halted at Market Street, where fish
were given to all the women. The
catch was prophetic of the luck of
Flood and O'Brien; they became
great barons of the Comstock
Bonanza and of stock and finance.

"...as everyone knows,
miner's luck is some-
thing like a fisherman's."
A.H Dexter

The Old Gray Eagle

Colonel/Senator Edward Baker & the California Regiment of the Pennsylvania 71st Infantry Regiment of old Californians; his great speeches had won California for his boyhood friend Lincoln as President. As a Senator from Oregon, he would have lost his seat if he accepted command of the Army. Here he leads his men at the awful battle of Ball's Bluff, early in the Civil War, October 21, 1861.

Captain Crowninshield, responsible for our cover, was here too.

COLONEL CONNOR & THE 3rd
CALIFORNIA INFANTRY Rgt.,
Nevada & Utah, 1862

Blue flag, gold stars, fringe, letters, eagle. Red scrolls, stripes in shield. Dark blue coats, light blue trim and trousers.

E PLURIBUS UNUM

3ª REGT.
INFANTRY
C.V.

Union Blue
Uniforms

The Territory of Nevada was founded in 1861, and it soon quarreled with California over their boundary. Fighting began in Susanville. It was Civil War time, and Col. Connor and the 3rd Infantry of California Volunteers took command. "Traitors shall not utter treasonable sentiments in this district," he said.

BEAR REPUBLIK

BEARS

THE BEAR REPUBLIC

KNIGHTS OF THE GOLDEN CIRCLE

Old red house

"The people of California should all be of one mind on this subject of a Pacific Republic. Raise aloft the flag of the hydraheaded cactus of the western wilds and call upon the enlightened nations of the earth to acknowledge our independence and protect us from the wreck of a once glorious Union." — Congressman Jn. Burch, *S.F. Herald*, Jan. 3, 1860. However: "California cherishes a loyal devotion to the union. Our honor and our pride are in its flag...California repudiates the suggestion of a Pacific republic." State Senator DeLong, 1861.

El Monte was the home of old Texans, all determined secessionists. The Bear Flag, banner of break-away government, was painted and paraded there by about 200 of their Home Guard around patriotic Jonathan Tibbett's house. Many people had favored California with Oregon, etc., becoming a new country, the Pacific Republic, to weaken the north.

PACIFIC REPUBLIC

The Texas Confederates took New Mexico and Arizona; it was feared they would continue on to California, to be joined by many secessionists here. The California Column, about 1,500 men under Col. Carleton, was oranized to recapture New Mexico and Arizona. Carleton's own 1st Infantry and the 1st Cavalry made up a large part of the Column.

General Sibley's rebels held Albuquerque and Santa Fe. The Cal. Column trod eastward across the Great Desert; Sibley, hearing of their approach, evacuated the country. Tucson was retaken on May 12, 1862. Then on to Texas went the California troops.

GENERAL CARLETON AND THE CALIFORNIA COLUMN, 1862

Union Blue Uniforms

1st INFANTRY C.V.

The flag is in the State Capitol, Sacramento

"I send you a set of colors which have been borne by this Column. They were hoisted by Col. West on Forts Breckenridge and Buchanan, and over Tucson, Ariz.; by Col. Eyre over Forts Thorn, Fillmore, and over Mesilla, N. Mex., and over Fort Bliss in Texas. They were hoisted by Capt. Cremony over Fort Quitman, and by Capt. Shirland over Fort Davis, in Texas, and thus again have those places been consecrated to our beloved country." *Gen. Carleton*

See Orton, *Records of Cal. Men in the War of the Rebellion*, 1890

A HUGE OLD GLORY

Southern California was Southern in sympathy and 'Dixie' was the only tune heard anywhere ("dogs bark it, asses and mules bray it"). So the Los Angeles Unionists held a Grand Union rally. They met in the plaza; the Army Band played, Mr. Banning gave a roaring speech and a giant U.S. flag. We were now pro-Union.

SLAVERY — IS — WRONG! -ABE

THE UNION FOREVER

Union Blue Uniforms

Daily Alta California

Dec. 11, 1862

REVIEW OF THE CALIFORNIA HUNDRED

Captain Reed's cavalry company of California Rangers, or as they are at present, and will be in the future, best known, "The California Hundred," were reviewed on the Plaza (Portsmouth Square) yesterday afternoon, by Mayor Teschemacher and other prominent citizens. They were also inspected by Lieut Col. Thomson, after which they paraded through the principal streets and returned to the headquarters at Assembly Hall. The company were presented yesterday with a fine guidon by D. Norcross, Esq. It is composed of white and crimson silk, having the letters U.S. in gilt over a California grizzly bear, which latter we presume, will be adopted as an appropriate emblem by the troop. It will not be the first time that the "Bear Flag" has been borne on the battlefield. The guidon is beautifully mounted, and reflects great credit upon Mr. Norcross' taste in getting it up in the nick of time, and his liberality in bestowing it upon the gallant fellows who are to carry it when doing battle for the Union. A visit to their barracks showed that they were all in readiness for their departure to the East, by the steamer *Golden Age* today. Blankets, overcoats, trunks and travelling sacks were piled in order: and some few, who are disposed to "be jolly" under all circumstances, carry with them musical instruments, with which to beguile the monotony of the sea voyage. A lighter and more serviceable sabre than that now used (by the kindness of the First Light Dragoons) will be provided them on their arrival at their destination, Boston... The "Hundred" will be escorted to the steamer this morning by the Vallejo Rifles, Captain Frisbie, (which company arrived last evening), the Light Dragoons, Kidd's Brass Band of 20 pieces, and a Committee of citizens...May they have a prosperous voyage and have an early chance to distinguish themselves as California horsemen upon the battlefield, and the day will come when that grizzly guidon will take its place as one of Califoronia's proudest mementoes of the times that tried men's love for the Union.

Men from the country will be preferred.

Green uniforms here; blue hereafter

Guidon: red & white stripes, gold letters; State Capitol Sacramento

The CALIFORNIA HUNDRED
J. Henry Rogers, 1865

First for his country, in her need
For volunteers, was Sewell Reed...
"Dear one, I've gathered in our land
To go with me, a gallant band.
Thousands stood forth, at my request,
To represent the golden West;
But from each thousand warlike men,
My limit was to choose but ten.
And from their sturdy ranks I took
One hundred men,—each had a look
Of desp'rate courage in his eyes; ...

A new recruit is speaking now
With laughing eye and sunny brow;
She whispers in my listening ear:
"Come, take one female volunteer!"
"'Tis well, I'll keep thee by my side,
With my brave 100 thou shalt ride..."
With Freedom's banner is unrolled,
The standard from the land of gold.

We, like our patriot sires of yore,
Will bear the flag they nobly bore—
But on our banner now appears
A stain, which darker grows with years,
And freemen must this stain efface,
And no distinction make of race,
Nor name, nor color; each must hold
His liberty, at price untold...
The land where Freedom's flag unrolls;
Kings trembled when they saw unfurl'd
The motto - 'Freedom to the world;' ...
Uniforms: blue

The Massachusetts Pine Tree was mixed
with the California Bear because Captain
Sewell Reed and his wife Harriet, Yankees
from Massachusetts before they settled in
Alameda, joined their troop of California Hundred Rangers with the 2nd
Massachusetts Cavalry, where good riders
were needed. California's were the best!
Poet John Henry Rogers, writer of the
immortal epic *The California Hundred,*
was also a dedicated Yankee in California.

Rev. King's church friends in Charlestown, Mass.,
gave a party for the Cal. 100 Jan. 13, 1863.
Abbie Lord presented a big Old Glory (now in
Sacramento) which Capt. Reed's
flag-bearer surely saluted, too.

Walter Reed,
age 2

Hattie Reed, 30
flag bearer

Capt. J. Sewell Reed, 31
d. Feb. 22, 1863

FIRST GRAND REVIEW, POTOMAC'S GLORIOUS ARMY, April 9, 1863, Falmouth, Virginia

The coming troop their standard show'd
Its silken folds of fleecy white
Waved gaily in the fading light;
And on its field a pine-tree made
An evergreen and constant shade:
While underneath its boughs o'green
A grizzly bear was sleeping
seen...

That flag was from the land of gold;
In that white field, to them one said,
Was purity of purpose read;
An emblem in the pine was seen
Of friendly memories evergreen;
The monster, peaceful in his strength,
Reposing on the ground at length,
Might say: "The foes who wake my ire
In my embrace will soon expire;"
There friendship, truth, and strength unite
Their virtues in the field of white:
And in the silver border 'round it,
The word, "Eureka," I have found it.

"The enemy shall have no leisure."
President Lincoln
Gentle, plain, just and resolute, un-
der whose cautious hand, against
the foulest crime in history known
in any land or age, was saved the
Union of these States.
Walt Whitman

Strange was the flag, still stranger seem'd
The small hand in which it gleame'd:
And much they marvelled, one so fair
And young, their battle-flag should
bear, for all among the stranger band
Wore sunburnt face, roughen'd hand,
All, save the youthful standard-bearer...
Brave Sewell saw the varying streak
That flushed, then faded from her cheek.
He said, "Be firm, that none may know
A woman's heart beats soft below
That warlike dress; we'll soon meet eyes
I fear thy secret will surprise."

Liberty, won by our fathers...
tis ours to gild the letters and
to make them shine
with gold. *Blake*

Then from the ranks rode Sewell Reed
And bade his standard-bearer ride,
And bear their banner by his side...

Can this be she...
the goddess of
the sword and shield? *Bret Harte*

The chieftain questioned Sewell Reed,
Of him who proudly wav'd the silken Bear...
"Curious," he said, "it seem'd & strange
That one so young and fair, should range
From sweet home in some quiet glen,
And roam amongst those warlike men;
Yet stranger still that form so slight,
Should bear their banner in the fight.
But for his dress and martial mein,
And war-fire in his brown eye seen,
I'd risk the honor of my blade,
Thy standard-bearer is a maid.
'Tis acted well, her bearing bold,
I honor much her purpose high,
But beauty hath her secret told,
Giving her warlike dress the lie.
It shows deep feeling for our cause,
When from the fire-side it draws
A lovely woman, in disguise,
To fight where our brave banner flies.
Our arms must win when maid or wife,
Thus to her country gives her life
and victory round our standard play.

"My Dragoon force..."
Gen. Hooker

On Gen. Hooker's plan:
"Our prime object is the enemies'
army in front of us."..*Pres. Lincoln,* April 9, 1863

And coming time will shed a golden glory
Around the mem'ry of Sewell Reed.

THE CALIFORNIA VOLUNTEER
INFANTRY IN THE CIVIL WAR

Flags in the Capitol,
Sacramento

17,000 Californians volunteered for the Union army. Colonel Carleton commanded the
1st Regiment, which assembled in Oakland in 1861, camped by Los Angeles, then marched
to San Diego and then to Fort Yuma. From there the California Column retook New Mexico.
The 2nd Regiment was at San Francisco, Santa Barbara and Fort Humboldt. The 3rd was at
Stockton, then went to Utah to protect the overland mail. The 4th, from Sacramento and the
gold country, served in Oregon and Southern California. The 5th reinforced the California
Column. The 6th was at Benicia and Humboldt; the 7th, from Sacramento and Marysville,
went to Yuma, and the 8th, raised in San Francisco and San Jose, served in California.

A SECOND REVIEW of
The GRAND ARMY
May 24, 1865
I read last night of
The Grand Review
In Washington's
Chiefest Avenue, —
Two hundred thousand
Men in Blue
I think they said was
The number...

The martyred heroes
of Malvern Hill
Of Gettysburg and
Chancellorsville,
The men whose
wasted figures fill
the patriot graves
of the nation...

(600,000 lost,
700,000 ill and
wounded)

Till I seemed to hear their trampling feet,
The bugle blast and the drum's beat,
The clatter of hoofs in the stony street,
The cheers of people who came to greet,
And the thousand details that to repeat
Would only my verse encumber,
Till I fell in a reverie, sad and sweet,
And then to a fitful slumber...

...And I saw a phantom army come
With never a sound
of fife or drum,
But keeping time to
a throbbing hum
Of wailing and
lamentation.

And there came
the nameless
dead, the men
Who perished
in fever, swamp
and fen, The
slowly-starved
of the prison-pen...
Bret Harte

THE PAIUTE
WAR & CHIEF
JOAQUIN
JIM
1862-67

US

Co. D.
2ND. CAV.CAL.
VOL.

PRESENTED TO THE

TUOLUMNE RANGERS

BY THE LADIES OF

SONORA.

"NEVER SURRENDER."

The winter of 1861-62 was terrible. The freezing Paiutes considered the whites as intruders, and to keep from starving, felt justified in taking the ranchers' cattle. But shootings for this followed, and there were scalpings in retaliation. So a treaty was signed—but Chief Joaquin Jim of the Southern Mono from Fresno was not at the signing. So more cattle were taken, and more shootings. A campaign against the Paiutes was organized; a campfire was surrounded, and many unsuspecting Paiutes were shot. Joaquin Jim could not agree to being dominated by the white men. He was determined and courageous. About 2,000 Paiutes met in the valley, and Capt. Kellog took a company to meet the warriors at Bishop Creek. The sheriff of Mono was killed and the whites retreated to Big Pine. Col. Evans and the Second California Cavalry came up from Los Angeles with Agent Wasson to try to make peace. The soldiers were fired on, a retreat was ordered, and Paiute confidence rose. "They will fight to the last in defense of their homes," said the agent. The Paiutes took back all of Owens Valley in 1862. Gen. Wright sent out the "Mono and Owens River Military Expedition" with 157 men. On July 4, 1862 they raised the U.S. flag at Camp Independence there.

Orders were to kill all the natives they saw. But the Paiutes wanted peace. A treaty was again made, with a fandango. Gold was found nearby, and now miners destroyed the grass seed which had fed the Paiutes. Joaquin Jim was hostile. A great pow-wow was held in September, on the Kern River, and war was decided upon. Everyone prepared for battle. A fight began at Cottonwood Creek, and many Paiutes fell. On the Kern River, they gave up their arms and then were shot down in cold blood by the soldiers. Company D on the Owens River rode about shooting Paiutes as they found them, and Company L went out to destroy their provisions at Bishop Creek. Peace negotiations again took place; "Paiutes were fired upon by some chivalrous miners, though they were unarmed and bore a white flag," said the *Esmeralda Star,* July 30. Soon 908 Paiutes were sent to Fort Tejon—if they refused to go the soldiers were to shoot them. The white flag left by the slaughtered Paiutes was taken away by Joaquin Jim, who substituted "his own war banner, a scarlet cloth bordered with raven feathers—said to have been a handsome piece of work." "Joaquin Jim has never been conquered. He has said frequently that he would not let the whites occupy his domain," worried a member of the next expedition. Shootings and skirmishes continued, and a crushing blow on the unsuspicious natives was determined upon at Owens Lake. Ruthless slaughter in the Paiute villages followed the "cry for extermination." "I never saw such inveterate haters," a citizen wrote. The chiefs met Capt. Noble of the Second Cavalry and offered him "all the wealth of their nation if he would leave Round Valley and take away his banner of stars."

U.S. Flags: State Capitol, Sacramento
See W.A. Chalfant, *The Story of Inyo,* 1922

A BRAVE WOMAN WITH FLYING COLORS, LASSEN, 1864

A fancy-looking fellow rides up an' sez he: "Cap, take a fool's advice an' haul down your dish-rag. This is a secesh camp."
Pop, he fires up and says, "Stranger, if you're spilin' for a diffikilty you kin hev it here. The first man that lays a hand on that flag, *I'll drop him sure!*" Chiv he looked black, but Pop had his turkey-buster well in hand, and Chiv changed his base and fell back. Pop cracked his black-snake and we all rid into the secesh camp with flying colors and all of us, big an' little, peeked out of the wagon and give 'em as we rid along the main street, 'Rally round the flag, boys, rally round the flag.'

"Folks say Californy's the best country. I don't know. It ought to be a good country, for it takes a dreadful long time to get to it, and costs a pile of money."

J. Ross Browne,
Harper's Monthly,
June, 1866

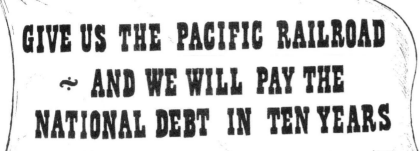

GIVE US THE PACIFIC RAILROAD ~ AND WE WILL PAY THE NATIONAL DEBT IN TEN YEARS

Ha! A flag celebrating Lincoln's reelection, flown March 4, 1865, Camp Douglas *Vedette* next day: cited in Fred Rogers, *Soldiers of the Overland*, 1938, p. 140.

"We have prayed and sighed for a railroad. . . If, four years ago, we had elected Frémont, in four months after, he would have recommended a railroad," speechified Col. Baker in 1859. "We are running a man now by the name of Lincoln (cheers) who will do the same thing. . . If he recommends a railroad—and he will—he won't twaddle about it." And he didn't. Engineer Judah determined that a railroad could be built over the Sierra Nevada mountains, and then persuaded these Sacramento shopkeepers of Lincoln's party to set up the company to do it. A road in the direction of the great

THE SACRAMENTO FOUR

Mark Hopkins, Treasurer

We have served California.
C. P. Huntington, V.P.

The children of California will be my children.
Governor Stanford, Pres.

I can build a mile a day.
C. Crocker
Indeed he could, with a brave army of 12,000 hardy Chinese workers.

Monogram: gold leaf and medium green

silver bonanza would be very rewarding, they noted. Judah next persuaded Congress to support construction as a "war measure₁ Two companies were to₂ build the road, the Union Pacific from the Missouri River westward, and the Central Pacific of these gents from Sacramento east.—

The two lines met at Promontory, Utah, May 10, 1869. The Southern Pacific RR was begun in 1865, running south from Gilroy.

These four were "men of remarkable enterprise and administrative talent . . . to their boldness is due, in no small measure, the greatness and prosperity of this our western commonwealth."
—*Bancroft*

Flag: see the Calaveras *Californian*, May 6, 1948. "Despite the failure of Senator Jesse M. Mayo's resolution presented to the State Senate to replace the golden bear with the jumping frog, on the official state flag, it will be the frog—not the bear—who flies on the flag that will wave over Frog Town May 14, 15, 16, during the Calaveras Centennial Fair and Jumping Frog Jubilee . . ."

"California's bear has been chiefly employed in disturbing prospectors, sacking hen roosts, frightening women and children, while the frog has greatly enriched the world's literature." —Senator Jesse M. Mayo,1948

LITERARY CALIFORNIA*
Mark Twain, 1865

CALIFORNIA REPUBLIC

One day Sam Clemens had to leave San Francisco in a hurry, and went to live up at Jackass Hill, and from there went to Angels Camp. There he got the story, wrote it up and sent it to Artemus Ward in New York; he gave it to the *Saturday Review,* where it appeared November 18, 1865. It is about Jim Smiley's frog Dan'l Webster: He "can outjump any frog in Calaveras County" said Smiley to a stranger, as $40 was bet that he could. Smiley went to find a frog for the stranger, while he, holding Smiley's frog, took out a teaspoon and "filled him pretty near up to his chin" with quail shot. Smiley soon returned and handed the stranger his frog. "Now, if you're ready, set him alongside of Dan'l...one, two, three, Git...the new frog hopped off lively, but Dan'l gave a heave...but it warn't no use...the feller took the money and started away...'I do wonder what in the nation that the frog throw'd off for...he 'pears to look mighty baggy, somehow...why bless my cats if he don't weigh five pounds'—and turned him upside down and he belched out that double handfull of shot...he was the maddest man...and took out after that feller, but he never ketched him." To celebrate, a jumping frog Jubilee began in 1928, and had its own flag in 1948.

THE MOJAVE ROAD: LOS ANGELES TO ARIZONA, 1867

Battles with the Paiutes were frequent on the road in the vast desert between San Bernardino and the Colorado River, and the new U.S. Mail line in 1867 needed protection. Co. B of the new 8th Regt. of U.S. Cavalry, recruited entirely in California, went to Camps Cady and Rock Spring, mail relay stations on the Mojave Road. Then the army began shifting troops around the desert, as men were needed in tough Arizona.

Blue regimental flag; blue uniforms.
See D. Casebier, *Camp Rock Spring*, 1973

Union Blue
Uniforms

The cavalry at these camps would be replaced by Co. K of the 14th Regt. of the U.S. Infantry. The foot soldiers would protect the mail, two mails each week in each direction; one soldier would ride in every mail buggy. On the road, "war with the Hualpais began by the murder of their chief by a party of whites," reported the *Alta California*, Oct. 29; the usual sad story.

In 1874 the Women's Crusade and the temperance movement boomed across the land. The Woman's Suffrage movement had been going for a few years, and many of its leaders were active in the temperance movement, too. An important anti-liquor election was held in San Jose, and Sallie Hart, a fiery red-headed suffragette "with a tongue like a scorpion," bravely speechified against howling mobs of liquor men. A band of fifty small children paraded past the polls (where only men could vote), singing the famous songs and urging votes for cleaner living. The liquormen grew nasty; Sallie made speech after speech. The men got violent; Sallie was saved by the police. Though her cause that day was lost, the foe provided ample reason for future victory. A week later she rallied in Alameda: "The rum power," wrote the San Francisco *Post,* "looked with astonishment and then with alarm on the new crusade...and trembled at the new and potent force which came into the field, when women put their hands to the work." "One very unexpected result... is the creation of a sentiment favorable to female suffrage. We hear of persons who have always opposed it, who responded to Miss Sallie Hart's challenge."

TEMPERANCE

FATHER, DEAR FATHER COME HOME WITH ME NOW

Local Option
WOMAN'S SUFFRAGE
1874 Crusade

Why should not I—American born, have as good a right to come here and exert an influence in behalf of what I believe to be just, as you?

SALOON KEEPERS ASSOC. FOREVER

San Jose *Mercury,* June 23, 26, 1874; San Francisco *Bulletin,* June 30, July 2, 1874; G. Ostrander, *The Prohibition Movement in California,* 1957.

DENNIS KEARNEY & THE WORKINGMEN'S PARTY

The gold mines stalled in 1865, the Central Pacific Railroad was done, the Bank of California closed, the stock market crashed. With little rain, farming died. Thousands came to City Hall in San Francisco to hear Irish Dennis Kearney shout up the Workingman's Party. But his speeches killed business; then rain came back, and with it prosperity. Dennis becme a rich real estate broker. God bless America.

Red flag, red beard on J.C. Day, vice-president; ship flags: Coleman's California Line, left, blue top and bottom, red sides', white center; Henry W. Peabody's Line, right, white flag, red letter

WORKINGMEN'S PARTY OF CALIFORNIA

Thieves, peculators, landgrabbers, bloated bond-holders, railroad magnates and shoddy aristocrats.

Labor of male and female, where of equal value, must be equally compensated.

CALIFORNIA & REAL ESTATE THE BOOM OF 1887

Flag: see J. Wilson, *Wolfskill*, 1965. See T. Van Dyke, *Millionaires of a Day*, 1890

The rate war between Southern Pacific and Santa Fe Railroads in 1887 - Kansas to Los Angeles cost only a dollar; emigrants weary of the bad eastern weather; Nordhoff's book, *California for Health, Pleasure & Residence,* 1873; the tricks of old-time boomers from the Midwest, the promise for citrus growing; shameless boomer advertising; all this made the world maniacal for Southern California land. An example was the sale of Wolfskill's Orchard Tract in Los Angeles, by the river. Some acres were given to S.P for a railroad station, which made the rest of the land wildly popular. Lots right in the river were sold for huge sums by the Los Angeles Land Bureau, a boom outfit. They also sold land in West Los Angeles, bought at $10 an acre in 1884 and sold for $100 an acre in 1887, to the Santa Monica Land Co. "Fully five-sixths of the buyers were buying, not for use, but to sell at an advance to someone else in a few days or weeks...But the worst mistake was ignoring the immense amount of fine land and fine climate in Southern California, the supply of which must inevitably break any market." And, poof! The boom busted. But we've had many more fine booms since. More will come.

"Fiddlesticks! This country is good for nothing but climate."

WOLFSKILL LOTS For Sale.
BRANCH OFFICE LOS ANGELES LAND BUREAU
EASTON, ELDRIDGE & CO.| Geo W. FRINK, President

WOLFSKILL TRACT for Private Sale

"The race of real estate buyers are the silliest of sheep, and need leading."

"One fool makes many."

"I do not propose taking a lifetime to get rich."

"The purity of the air of Los Angeles is remarkable."

CALIFORNIA & THE U.S. NAVY
Mare Island & the Spanish-American War, 1898

It was men of the Navy ashore who took California in 1846; even Frémont's Battalion was under Navy orders. Next a navy yard for the Pacific Squadron was needed. Mare Island near Vallejo, which had belonged to General Vallejo, seemed to be the spot. President Fillmore reserved the island for the Navy, and Commodore Sloat and a naval board liked the site. The first commander, David Farragut, took command on Sept. 16, 1854, and on Oct. 3, Old Glory was first raised there. A floating dry dock came around the horn, and our ships were soon being repaired there. The docks of the the Pacific Mail Steamship Co. were at Benicia nearby, and their big ships began to use the Navy drydocks, too. The *Independence*, "Old Ironsides," arrived in 1855, and stayed for 70 years. The U.S.Navy wasn't large in those days. In 1860 we had only 90 ships; half were out of commission. During the Civil War the fleet reached 700 ships . With peace, it went down to 185 ships in 1871, and 139 in 1881. Mare Island grew or shrank with the size of the fleet. In 1898 the *Maine* was sunk in Havana, and "the belligerent old turtle" U.S.S. *Monadnock*, below, left the island for the Philippines on Apr. 22 as Pres. McKinley declared war. From her signal yard read *"Remember the Maine."* This interesting Monitor had been under construction from 1876 to 1896 - the second ship built at Mare Island other than two tugs. During the World Wars, Mare Island's shipyard built and repaired fleets of cruisers, destroyers, submarines, tenders, tankers and transports. The *Pennsylvania*, our first aircraft carrier, was built there; 40,000 workers were at the yard during WWII, to keep the fleet afloat. They had much to do with winning the war. They built 386 ships and they made 70,000 flags each month during the war.

U.S.S. *Monadnock*, 1898

CALIFORNIA AND THE UTOPIAN COMMUNITIES: Katherine Tingley the "Lotus Mother" and the Universal Brotherhood, Point Loma, San Diego, 1890—1929

See *Unversal Brotherhood Path,* April, 1900; thanks to Kirby van Mater of the Theosophical Society for having gotten out this flag for us. "I'm very disappointed in this flag," he said, "because it is much brighter than Mrs. Tingley would have approved of."

Flag: Purple and gold stripe; purple canton, gold devices. Purple dress.

RAJA YOGA SCHOOL

68793245
X 76721348
550345,960

California has had many interesting communities searching for better lives. Most have failed. An example is Mrs. Tingley's Universal Brotherhood, opened at Point Loma in 1897, "for the benefit of humanity and the glory of ancient sages." It was Theosophical, or "divine wisdom," the movement begun by Mme Blavatsky, the modern priestess of Isis. Soon there were hundreds of people at Point Loma; half were children in the Raja Yoga School. The Isis League of Music & Drama there produced lots of Shakespeare, often for the sailors of San Diego. This really must have been Utopia.

ITALIAN CALIFORNIA

San Francisco in 1904 was our largest Italian settlement, and A.P. Giannini would soon make it prosperous. His Bank of Italy opened in 1904, to serve the "little fellow."

We are going to rebuild San Francisco and it will be better than ever.

Months later, San Francisco shook apart; A.P.'s bank promptly helped put it back together. The other greatest Italian since Augustus, Caruso, just happened to be in San Francisco on April 18, 1906, about to sing in a benefit for the victims of an eruption of Mt. Vesuvius. But the San Andreas fault's bouncing destroyed the opera house and 28,000 other buildings. It also shook the great tenor "'Ell of a place," he said. "I never come back."

RUMBLE RUMBLE

BANCA D'ITALIA

BANK OF ITALY

BANK OF ITALY
BANCA D'ITALIA

BANK OF ITALY

Teddy Roosevelt
TR

Flag of the Kingdom of Italy: green, white, red tricolor; red shield with the white cross of Sàvoy, surrounded by a blue border. The bank's customers complained if the Italian tricolor wasn't flown when they thought it should be. *Cal. Hist. Soc. Quarterly,* September, 1968.

Note: A.P.'s father was from a village near Genoa and settled in San Jose, where A.P. was born in 1870. Caruso escaped the earthquake with a prized autographed photograph of President Roosevelt. He had felt his bed rocking like a boat at 5:00 A.M. He looked out the window, saw buildings toppling, and was soon seen wandering downtown in pajamas and a fur coat.

CALIFORNIA & ADVENTURE: JACK & CHARMIAN LONDON ON THE *SNARK*, 1907

Californians are adventurers by nature. It was for adventure that we or our ancestors came here in the first place. Jack London not so long ago was our national adventurer; everyone read his books about derringdo. Charmian, his wife, was an adventurer first class, too. When the Londons left Oakland on their 57' ketch *Snark*—named after Mr. Lewis Carroll's poem—they flew at the masthead Jimmy Hopper's first Varsity sweater. Hopper was a great footballer at Berkeley then; this flag represented extreme good luck.

"And we go - go - go away from here!
On the other side the world we're overdue!"

I am sure we ought to thank Mr. Kipling
for contributing largely to our undauntedness.

"And I'd sell my tired soul
for the bucking beam-sea roll ..."

Sweater: Blue & Gold; sea: purple
See C. London, *The Log of the Snark*, 1915.

CALIF ORNIA

PIC TURE

COM PANY

BEARS

GO CAL

The movie business was once California's greatest glory. In the sunshine of Southern California—perfect for shooting outdoors scenes—a Scots gent, Robert Brunton, in about 1913 found an empty barn for a studio on Sunset Boulevard, surrounded by oak or "holly" trees. There he put Mack Sennett to work. Soon, Jesse Lasky and his sister Blanche hired young Cecil B. DeMille to film in the neighborhood, and Hollywood had become movieland. Then the hilariousHarold Lloyd arrived; he is shown here with the masthead flag of *The Freshman,* filmed during an actual game up in the Berkeley stadium in 1924. How much joy Hollywood has given the world is incalculable.

Flag colors: Blue and Gold, of course, even though the movie was black-and-white.

WINKIE — MUNCHKIN
GILLIKIN — QUADLING

* He took the name from
from his file cabinet, O - Z.

"How lucky we were to discover this beautiful country," exclaimed Trot in *The Scarecrow of Oz*, (1915, Ch. 9). "The country seems rather high class, I'll admit, Trot," said Cap'n Bill. "No one could live in such a country without being happy and good," added Trot, who was a true California girl. And California is where Mr. Baum had moved when he wrote these words and ten of the fourteen wonderful books of Oz.* He had written successful plays, done Shakespeare, raised chickens, dealt in oil, gone broke, become a Dakota merchant, gone broke, moved to Chicago, written for a newspaper, turned travelling salesman (crockery), started a magazine, and rooted for the Cubs.

He'd surely end up in California. And all along he told lots of children lots of truly delightful stories. "Write them down," said his mother-in-law, and he did; in 1900 *The Wonderful Wizard of Oz* appeared and was a sudden best seller.

Flag: "They played the National air called 'The Oz Spangled Banner,' and behind them were the standard bearers with the Royal flag. This flag was divided into four quarters, one being colored sky-blue, another pink, a third lavender and a fourth white. In the center was a large emerald-green star, and all over the four quarters were sewn spangles that glittered beautifully in the sunshine. The colors represented the four countries of Oz, and the green star the Emerald City."
—*Dorothy and the Wizard in Oz*, (1908, Ch. 17

The next two Oz books were written in Michigan; the fourth, *Dorothy and the Wizard in Oz*, was written in Coronado, California, where the Baums wintered in 1907/8. This book had a California setting, with an earthquake like San Francisco's of 1906. Mr. Baum wrote nine more Oz books in California, as well as dozens of others. But his first love was the stage; the first Oz books had been made into a wonderful operetta, and made Mr. Baum rich. Other ventures failed, and broke him. His stories were handy for the new medium—the movies. Baum hired Selig and his Polyscope machine in 1908 to make a movie of *The Land of Oz*. Mr. Baum narrated while an orchestra made music; his eldest son was the projectionist. This lost money, too. The Baums, though, like all of us, preferred California to anywhere else, anyway. So here they came for good. They moved to 149 N. Magnolia Avenue in Los Angeles—"never had any city in any fairyland ever equalled this one in stately splendor," he wrote (*Scarecrow in Oz*, Ch. 21). Soon after they bought a lot at 1749 Cherokee Avenue, Hollywood, and there they built Ozcot. Mr. Baum then noticed the new industry growing up in his neighborhood and formed the Oz Film Manufacturing Company with a studio on Santa Monica Boulevard. The first picture was *The Patchwork Girl of Oz*, five reels, and it failed too. "In life, nothing adverse lasts very long," he later wrote. After 1915 Mr. Baum stuck to writing Oz books, playing golf in Griffith's Park, raising Rhode Island reds, playing with Toto, his cocker spaniel, growing prize chrysanthemums, looking after his hundreds of beautiful birds, and corresponding with children. He died in 1919, midway between the California Gold Rush and today. In no make-believe land have such wonders ever happened as in these eras. He is buried in Forest Lawn in Glendale. In 1925 Oliver Hardy played *The Tin Woodman* in a film, and in 1939, MGM made their great masterpiece. Oz surely lives forever, and the closest thing to it is our California.

"Things had to be dreamed of before they became realities," said Mr. Baum. "So I believe that dreams . . . are likely to lead to the betterment of the world. The imaginative child will become the imaginative man or woman most apt to create, invent, and therefore to foster civilization." *The Lost Princess of Oz*, Preface

CALIFORNIA & SPORT
Frank Baum observes
California life, 1908

""Our boys...are never obligated to interrupt their game for lower branches of learning." —Woggle-Bug, T.E. in *Dorothy & the Wizard in Oz*, Ch. 17, Coronado, 1908.

Flags: *The Baum Bugle*, 1966

CHIEF ENGINEER WILLIAM MULHOLLAND

Young Mulholland arrived in Los Angeles in 1877 and worked on the *Zanja*—the water ditch of the town, pop. 9,000. At night he studied math and engineering, and Shakespeare for fun. By 1886 he was superintendent of the City Water Co. The city was growing and needed more water. In 1904 Mulholland found the Owens River, far to the north, full of "the purest snow water." After many battles, Owens River water would be brought to Los Angeles in an aqueduct running 250 miles down the Mojave Desert and by tunnel. The citizens of the Owens Valley were furious about losing their water, but President Teddy Roosevelt signed a Federal bill giving the water to Los Angeles. Five thousand men worked on the aqueduct. At the Elizabeth Tunnel, teams of "muckers" competed for a pennant and bonuses for the best distance dug. With the raising of Old Glory on Nov. 5, 1913, the great flow of water to Los Angeles began. Mulholland was asked to run for office: "I would rather give birth to a porcupine backwards than be mayor of Los Angeles," he said.

"What a revolting spectacle to meet on a one-way road!" - *Milkman Pinkerton*

"The big dam is busted!"

"The dam is broke; the dam is broke!"

California & Engineering:
OFFICER THORNTON, THE PAUL REVERE
OF THE ST. FRANCIS DAM BURST, 1928
Edwards was given a gold medal for bravery by the CHP.

Los Angeles needed to store more water, so engineer Mulholland built the St. Francis Dam near Saugus, in 1925. Cracks and leaks soon began after the reservoir was filled: the foundation was giving way! At 11:57P.M., March 12, 1928, the dam burst: a roaring wall of water 185 feet high blasted out. Down the Santa Clara Valley surged the wall. Thornton Edwards of the new Highway Patrol rode furiously to spread the alarm, to every third Santa Paula house and farm. The Red Cross came; the Boy Scouts came; and the wall of water came. There were more than 400 deaths. There would have been many more but for good Officer Thornton. "Don't blame anybody else," said Mulholland; "you just fasten it on me."

HAM & EGGS FOR CALIFORNIA: Sherman Bainbridge & the Pension Plan, 1938

"The screw ball" Robert Noble started the plan - "$25 Every Monday Morning." It was a wow, and homemade banners for it flew high above white heads everywhere. Sherman Bainbridge then led the movement, and here he speaks from his wheelchair at the Hollywood Bowl. Ham & Eggs got on the ballot - and lost. So old folks marched on Sacramento, singing "Glory Hallelujah." But Roosevelt's New Deal was going on, and the pension Ham & Eggers wanted they would soon have.

See: W. Moore, *Out of the Frying Pan*, 1939

"They call us Crack-Pots, and we are. We're going to crack their pots wide open."

LOS ANGELES, THE CITY WITH FOUR FLAGS IN HER SEAL

Lieutenant Josef Argüello, on the order of Governor Felipe de Neve, founded El Pueblo de Nuestra Señora la Reyna de los Angeles on September 4, 1781. The lovely name of the town (and early seals) suggest that she might be on the seal, with some cherubs. We provide the cherubs. This seal was designed in 1905 by the Assistant City Attorney, adopted March 2nd and approved on the 6th.

CITY OF LOS ANGELES

FOUNDED 1781

See Dawson's Catalogue 516, 1992, lot. 160

—attended by 176,466 Angelinos in ten days. Pilot Glen Curtis made the first successful flight on the Pacific Coast, 100 mph, two minutes aloft! Two ladies flew with pilot Pulham, "Wonder of Wonders!" It was a World Epic, and predicted Los Angeles would be the biggest spot in aviation, and very soon it was.

Dominguez Hills

POLISH CALIFORNIA: IGNACY JAN PADEREWSKI, PASO ROBLES RANCHER

He was one of the greatest pianists ever. The hot baths near Paso Robles were good for his sore arm, and he loved the beauty of the country. The Paderewskis bought the Ranchos San Ignacio and Santa Helena there. Once he was to play at San Jose, an appearance put on by Stanford student Herbert Hoover. The young man did not have all of the pianist's fee, so he gave him a note instead. When World War I came, Paderewski said, "I shall not play until Poland is free." In 1918, the war over, Paderewski became Prime Minister and went to the Peace Conference in Paris. Poland had 2.5 million homeless refugees and 2 million undernourished children. The U.S., through Herbert Hoover, sent food to the starving country—his debt more than repaid.

"One of Paderewski's great services to Poland was at the Peace Conference in Paris...[he] succeeded in enlarging the boundaries of Poland beyond the powers of the nation to assimilate the minorities they took in. They secured entirely too many fringes of Germans, Czechs, Russians and Lithuanians for the good of Poland," said Herbert Hoover. This was one of the causes of World War II.

GEORGE PATTON, Great General in World War II, was from Pasadena.
Here as Major General at the Desert Training Center, Indio, California, June, 1942

"War is a very simple thing, and the determining characteristics are self-confidence, speed and audacity."

Red flag, white stars

"Our success was primarily due to continued offensive...day and night...relentless and unceasing...and to the fact that we used maneuver. We held the enemy by the nose and kicked him in the pants..." Nov. 25, 1944

THE UNITED STATES MARINES TAKE OVER RANCHO SANTA MARGARITA Y LAS FLORES, 1942

In August, 1942, the Ninth U.S. Marine Regiment was ordered to march up from San Diego to establish their new Camp Pendleton, formerly the great Rancho Santa Margarita y Las Flores, 141,000 acres near Oceanside. On September 1, Lt. Col. Lemuel Shepherd (later Commandant of the Corps) and the Ninth set out; they arrived four days later, having fought simu- lated attacks all the way. Not long afterwards, Marines from Camp Pendleton fought the great Pacific battles of World War II. Many did not return.

Command Battle Standard (Type III, Class 1): red field and letters; gold emblem with silver seas; gold scrolls, fringe and tassels; Marine green uniforms; khaki webbing.

PRESIDENT HARRY S TRUMAN & THE FORMING OF THE UNITED NATIONS, SAN FRANCISCO, June 26, 1945

THE BEGINNING OF SILICON VALLEY
Bill Hewett & Dave Packard were students at Stanford of the great Electrical Engineering Professor Terman, the "Father of Silicon Valley." In 1939 they founded a company in a tiny garage at 367 Addison Ave., Palo Alto.

Their first big customer was Walt Disney! They made four oscillators for his movie *Fantasia*. They became perpetual innovators and were determined to contribute to society. The University was founded in 1885 by the Stanfords (see earlier in this) to honor their son, Leland, Jr., who died at age 15 while exploring Europe, and "to qualify its students for personal success & direct usefulness in life."

Red flag, white letters.

STANFORD

HEWLETT-PACKARD

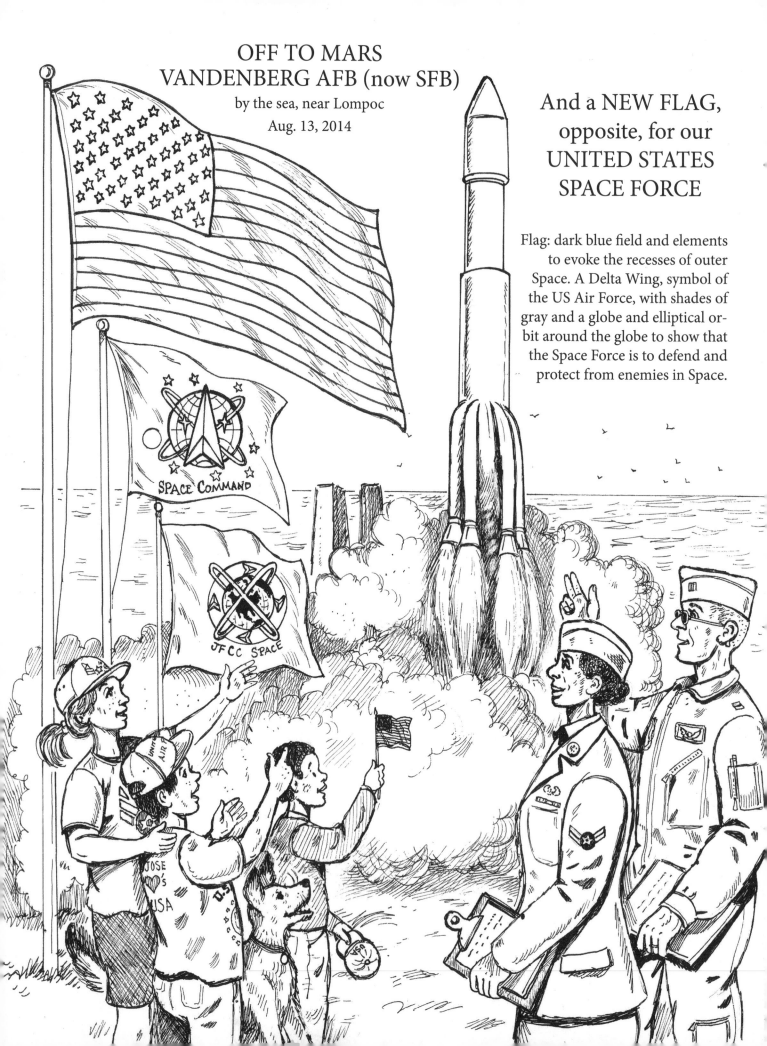